Specific Skill Series

Drawing Conclusions

Richard A. Boning

Fifth Edition

SRA/McGraw-Hill

Columbus, Ohio

To the Teacher

PURPOSE:
DRAWING CONCLUSIONS helps develop one of the most important interpretive skills. Pupils learn to look beyond the writer's literal statements to reach an unstated but logical conclusion based on those statements and sometimes their phrasing. In DRAWING CONCLUSIONS the correct conclusion is the most logical one for pupils to reach from only the information presented.

FOR WHOM:
The skill of DRAWING CONCLUSIONS is developed through a series of books spanning ten levels (Picture, Preparatory, A, B, C, D, E, F, G, H). The Picture Level is for pupils who have not acquired a basic sight vocabulary. The Preparatory Level is for pupils who have a basic sight vocabulary but are not yet ready for the first-grade-level book. Books A through H are appropriate for pupils who can read on levels one through eight, respectively. **The use of the *Specific Skill Series Placement Test* is recommended to determine the appropriate level.**

THE NEW EDITION:
The fifth edition of the *Specific Skill Series* maintains the quality and focus that has distinguished this program for more than 25 years. A key element central to the program's success has been the unique nature of the reading selections. Nonfiction pieces about current topics have been designed to stimulate the interest of students, motivating them to use the comprehension strategies they have learned to further their reading. To keep this important aspect of the program intact, a percentage of the reading selections have been replaced in order to ensure the continued relevance of the subject material.

In addition, a significant percentage of the artwork in the program has been replaced to give the books a contemporary look. The cover photographs are designed to appeal to readers of all ages.

SESSIONS:
Short practice sessions are the most effective. It is desirable to have a practice session every day or every other day, using a few units each session.

To the Teacher

SCORING:

Pupils should record their answers on the reproducible worksheets. The worksheets make scoring easier and provide uniform records of the pupils' work. Using worksheets also avoids consuming the exercise books.

It is important for pupils to know how well they are doing. For this reason, units should be scored as soon as they have been completed. Then a discussion can be held in which pupils justify their choices. (The Integrated Language Activities, many of which are open-ended, do not lend themselves to an objective score; thus there are no answer keys for these pages.)

GENERAL INFORMATION ON *DRAWING CONCLUSIONS*:

The questions in DRAWING CONCLUSIONS do not deal with direct references; thus the answers do not use the same words as the paragraphs. On the Picture Level, the readers examine the picture for the correct answer. The Preparatory, A, and B levels contain primarily indirect references; that is, the answers are found in the paragraphs but with slightly different wording. Some easy conclusions are also included. As the books advance in challenge, there are more difficult conclusions, involving less obvious relationships. The conclusions also become more dependent on qualifying words such as "mostly," "all," "some," or "only."

In DRAWING CONCLUSIONS the readers are asked to find an example, note a contrast, generalize, see cause and effect relationships, detect a mood, see an analogy, identify a time or place relationship, make a comparison, or anticipate an outcome.

It is important that the teacher ask pupils to find in the paragraph the specific information relevant to the tentative conclusion. Then pupils must test the conclusion against the information provided. When the emphasis is placed on finding evidence to prove answers and when the pupils put themselves in roles of detectives, not only does their ability to draw conclusions rapidly improve, but they also have fun.

Pupils must know that a conclusion is a judgment made. It must be supported by strong evidence. In DRAWING CONCLUSIONS the correct answer is one that is either highly likely or certain.

Some alternate answer choices may be true. The answer that is accepted as correct, however, must not only be true but must have supportive evidence in the paragraph. The clue may hinge on a single word, involve a phrase or a sentence, or encompass the paragraph as a whole.

RELATED MATERIALS:

Specific Skill Series Placement Tests, which enable the teacher to place pupils at their appropriate levels in each skill, are available for the Elementary (Pre-1–6) and Midway (4–8) grade levels.

About This Book

A writer does not tell you everything in a story. Sometimes you need to figure out things that are not told. This is called **drawing a conclusion**. A conclusion is what you can tell from what the writer tells you.

Good readers draw conclusions as they read. They think about what the writer tells them. Read this story. Think about what you can tell from what the writer says. Try to draw a conclusion about Liz.

> Liz put on her new skates. She stood up on the ice. Her right foot went one way. Her left foot went another way. Liz fell down! "Not again!" she cried. "I was hoping that these new skates would help me stay up."

Did you figure out that Liz has fallen before? You can draw this conclusion from the clues the writer gives—such as the word *again*.

In this book, you will read short stories. For each story, choose the answer that tells what you can tell from reading the story. Remember to use clues in the story to draw a conclusion.

1.   Pam was on her way outside. She looked out at the dark gray sky. Then she went to her room to put on her raincoat, boots, and hat. Pam opened her umbrella as she stepped outdoors.

_____

2.   "I know what we need," said Ron. "We need a tree in our backyard. We could put one right here. It would help make the yard look pretty. Will you get us a tree, Mother?"

_____

3.   The twins saw a goat at the fair. "Do you want to milk the goat?" asked its owner. Both of the children made the warm milk run into the bucket. The twins were surprised that a goat could give milk.

_____

4.   Bob walked into the room. He saw Peg looking at him. Dot was looking too. Lee was looking at him. Father and Mother kept looking too. They all watched Bob.

1. From the story you can tell that—

    (A) **Pam wanted to play**

    (B) **the sun was shining**

    (C) **rain was coming down**

---

2. From the story you can tell that—

    (A) **Ron wants Lee to buy some books**

    (B) **there were no trees in the backyard**

    (C) **the yard was full of trees**

---

3. From the story you can tell that—

    (A) **cows are not the only animals that give milk**

    (B) **goats are hard to milk**

    (C) **the milk was cold**

---

4. From the story you can tell that—

    (A) **Dot and Bob went to a party**

    (B) **five people looked at Bob**

    (C) **no one looked at Bob**

1. "I want to paint a picture," said Les. "I want to paint a picture of my school. I have some red paint and I have some white paint. Will you give me some paper, Mother?"

---

2. There was a pie-eating contest. Tom was first. He was the first to eat his piece of pie. "I am not surprised," said Mother. "You are always first here, too. You are always the first to eat your pie!"

---

3. "Mother," said Ann, "I want to learn how to cook. Do you know what I need? I need a book. I need a book that will show me how to cook. That's what I need!"

---

4. "You must help me, Lee," said Mother. "I didn't get to the store. I didn't get the things for the party. You must help out. Please go to the store for me right away. Hurry."

1. From the story you can tell that—

   (A) Les saw the girls in the house

   (B) the school isn't very big

   (C) the school is red and white

---

2. From the story you can tell that—

   (A) Tom went to school

   (B) Tom was not a slow eater

   (C) Mother could not believe that Tom won

---

3. From the story you can tell that—

   (A) Jan helped feed the baby

   (B) Ann wants to learn something new

   (C) Ann knows how to cook

---

4. From the story you can tell that—

   (A) there will soon be a party

   (B) the party is a long way off

   (C) Lee looked all over for the dog

1. "Please shut that off," Mother said to Bill. "You have been watching those shows all morning. Now it's time to do something else. Would you like to play a game or read a book with me?"

---

2. The paper bag jumped. It jumped up and down. The children were scared. Les laughed. "Don't be afraid," said Les holding up the bag. "Look inside." Inside was a frog. It was making the bag jump!

---

3. "What were you saying, Father?" asked Tom. "Just as I came into the room you said something about a boat ride. Are we going to go for a boat ride? Is that what you were talking about?"

---

4. "Don't yell into my ear," said Jan. "You make my ears ring. You're only a foot away. Do you think that I can't hear? I can hear everything you say. I could hear you ten miles away."

1. From the story you can tell that—

    (A) Bill had been playing outside

    (B) Bill had been watching TV

    (C) Bill likes to read books

---

2. From the story you can tell that—

    (A) Les is afraid of frogs

    (B) Les did not know what was in the bag

    (C) the paper bag was not moving by itself

---

3. From the story you can tell that—

    (A) Lee could not find anything to eat

    (B) Tom didn't hear everything Father said

    (C) Tom jumped into the snow

---

4. From the story you can tell that—

    (A) the children are near each other

    (B) Jan can't hear very well

    (C) the children want to play in the yard

1. "Don't leave the back door open," said Father. "It costs enough to heat the house. I am not trying to heat the whole neighborhood. Shut the door, and please keep it shut."

_____

2. "Someone is talking," said Ms. Hill. "I didn't call on anyone. Put up your hand if you want to talk. I can see your hand. I'll call on you, but we must all take turns."

_____

3. "Pat," said Mother, "I think that you are the one to keep an eye on the baby for me. I have to go out. Don't let the baby get out of bed. I'll be back in no time at all."

_____

4. "I'll get the door open," said Ron. "I have a key." Ron looked in one pocket. The key wasn't there. Ron looked in another pocket. The key wasn't there. "Where could the key be?" asked Ron.

1. From the story you can tell that—

    (A) Father is happy

    (B) Father is angry with the neighborhood

    (C) someone has not been careful

---

2. From the story you can tell that—

    (A) Ms. Hill knows how to swim

    (B) a hand was not raised

    (C) no one talked at all

---

3. From the story you can tell that—

    (A) Mother thinks Pat can do the job

    (B) Mother wants the baby to play

    (C) Les gave Jan a penny

---

4. From the story you can tell that—

    (A) the door was painted green

    (B) Ron often kept the key in a pocket

    (C) Mother fell asleep in the big chair

1. "Here!" shouted Peg. "Catch the ball." She threw the ball to Sam. "Now throw it back," she said. "I like to play ball. I have something to tell you. I am going to be on the school team."

---

2. "What kind of tree is it?" asked Father. "Have you seen that kind of tree before? Look at the leaves, Les. Do the leaves look like the leaves of the tree in your backyard?"

---

3. "I know what I would like to be," said Rosa. "I would like to be a letter carrier. People would be happy to see me each day. It would be fun to walk around the town."

---

4. "I was talking first," said Pat. "Jan, when you have something to say, I wait for you to stop. I don't talk. You should do the same. You should wait for me to stop before you start talking."

1. From the story you can tell that—

   (A) Father gave Peg a ball

   (B) Peg was a good player

   (C) Sam did not like to play ball

2. From the story you can tell that—

   (A) Lee wanted to get into the ball game

   (B) all trees have the same kind of leaves

   (C) you can tell a tree by its leaves

3. From the story you can tell that—

   (A) Rosa wants to be a farmer

   (B) Rosa wants to see happy people

   (C) Bob and Rosa had their picture taken

4. From the story you can tell that—

   (A) Pat was angry with Jan

   (B) Jan liked her new bike

   (C) Pat was pleased with Jan

1. "Les, I can't see you," said Mother. "You said that you were in the picture. I can't see you at all. Where are you? Are you in the back row? Are you in the front?"

---

2. "Meet our paper carrier," said Mother. Sam and Ann looked. They did not see anyone. Then they saw Tag. The dog was coming to the door. It had the newspaper. It was holding the paper in its mouth.

---

3. "Did you hear what happened to our wagon?" asked the children after breakfast. "Someone took it from our yard. We saw it last night just after dinner. When we looked there this morning, the wagon was gone."

---

4. "Jan, you have been on the telephone too long," said Mother. "I want to call Father. I can't wait all day, Jan. How long are you going to talk? I must call soon."

1.   From the story you can tell that—

   (A) Lee worked all day in the house

   (B) Mother finds Les right away

   (C) Mother thinks Les knows the answer

2.   From the story you can tell that—

   (A) Father left on a trip

   (B) Mother is angry with Tag

   (C) Mother saw Tag first

3.   From the story you can tell that—

   (A) the wagon was taken at night

   (B) the wagon was very big

   (C) the children took a picture

4.   From the story you can tell that—

   (A) Jan wants Ron to come out

   (B) Mother is pleased with Jan

   (C) Mother is angry with Jan

A. Exercising Your Skill

Read the sentences. What can you tell that the writer does not say? On your paper answer the question.

> You see bats, balls, and gloves.
> You hear "Strike One!"
> You smell hot dogs.
> You taste peanuts.
> Where are you?

> You see a pile of presents.
> You hear children singing.
> You smell candles.
> You taste cake.
> Where are you?

B. Expanding Your Skill

Read the question, and think about it. Then write your answer on your paper. Tell why you answered each question the way you did.

1. Would you like to go to a ball park or an airport?
2. Would you like to go to a zoo or a library?
3. Would you like to go to a beach or a forest?
4. Would you like to go to a jungle or a farm?

On your paper, list other places you would like to visit.

C. Exploring Language

On your paper, draw lines and a circle for a map like the one below. (Do not write the words that are in this map.) In the circle, write a word that names one place that you would like to visit. Then add words that tell what you might see, hear, smell, or taste there.

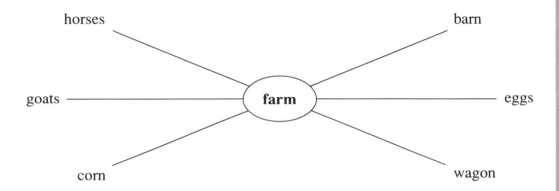

Now write sentences about the place you would like to visit. Use the words in your map.

D. Expressing Yourself

Here are some questions. Ask a friend or someone at home to answer them.

- What place do you like to visit?
- Why do you like that place?
- What can you see, hear, smell, or taste there?

Draw a picture showing the place that someone told you about. In the picture show what you learned about the place.

1. The children watched the train going by. "It's carrying many different things," they said. "Some cars are filled with food. Here come some cars with logs. See the cars with new tractors on them. Look at the cars filled with sheep and pigs!"

2. Mother put some seeds into a pan. They looked hard and shiny. What were they? "Wait a minute, Dot," she said. "You will see." Suddenly Dot heard a lot of noise. Mother was making popcorn!

3. "Oh," said Father. "I can't see where I'm going. It's raining so hard. I never saw it rain so hard. I must stop the car. I hope this doesn't keep up. When the rain lets up, I will go on."

4. "Come on, everyone," said Pat. "You can't catch me. You never could catch me. I can get away from you. No one will ever catch me. I can run fast. I can run faster than anyone here."

UNIT 7

1. From the story you can tell that—

   (A) the train carries only milk

   (B) the train is a long one

   (C) the sheep got lost

---

2. From the story you can tell that—

   (A) Dot's ears told her what the seeds were

   (B) the seeds were white and soft

   (C) Mother sent Dot to the store

---

3. From the story you can tell that—

   (A) Father is happy that it is raining

   (B) Father wants to be safe

   (C) Mother went on the train

---

4. From the story you can tell that—

   (A) the children had raced Pat before

   (B) Pat wasn't very fast

   (C) Lee could see Mother at the door

1.   "Look at the baby chickens," said the children. "They are going into the water. Stop them! They will drown." When the farmer laughed, the children said, "Oh, those are not chickens. They are baby ducks. They know how to swim."

---

2.   "It's so hot in here," said Jan. "I don't like it like this, Mother. I like it to be cool. I think that I will open the back door. That will help make it a little cooler."

---

3.   "Stop jumping, Biff," said José. "Biff, you need to be cleaned. How can I get you clean? You bad dog. You must help me. It won't take long. Soon you'll be clean."

---

4.   "Don't pick up that box alone," said Mother. "It is too heavy for you, Les. You are not big enough to pick it up. You will hurt yourself. Wait until I can help you. We will pick it up together."

1. From the story you can tell that—

    (A) the farmer thinks chickens can swim

    (B) the children know ducks can swim

    (C) the chickens went for a walk

2. From the story you can tell that—

    (A) Jan thinks it's too cold

    (B) Lee saw Jan in the yard

    (C) Jan is in the house

3. From the story you can tell that—

    (A) José is pleased with Biff

    (B) José is angry with Biff

    (C) José wants Biff to jump

4. From the story you can tell that—

    (A) Les is big and strong

    (B) Mother does not want Les to be hurt

    (C) Mother is happy

1. Lee said, "I wish I had a telephone in my room, Mother. You could call on the one downstairs. I could use the one up in my room. Then no one would have to wait."

_____

2. Ron got out a jar of peanut butter. He took two slices of bread. "Dad," he said, "I need a knife. I'd like some jelly, too."

_____

3. "Help!" cried Sam. "My toy boat is sailing away again." A girl in a big boat heard the cry. The girl went after the toy boat. She got it. She gave it back to Sam.

_____

4. "I am trying to take your picture," said Mother. "Stop moving, Les. Stop moving, Pat. Stay nice and quiet. Try to be like Jan. Jan can stand still in one place. If you move, I can't take your picture."

1. From the story you can tell that—

    (A) Mother made a new blue dress for Lee

    (B) sometimes Lee had to wait for the telephone

    (C) Lee didn't want a telephone of her own

2. From the story you can tell that—

    (A) Ron was feeding the dog

    (B) Ron knows how to make a sandwich

    (C) Ron and Dad were eating out

3. From the story you can tell that—

    (A) Mother went to work

    (B) the big boat was slower

    (C) this was not the first time Sam lost his boat

4. From the story you can tell that—

    (A) Jan was moving

    (B) Mother wanted the picture to turn out well

    (C) Les and Pat were helping Mother

1. "Sit down, children," said Mother. "You didn't eat all of your food. You can't get up and walk away. You must eat everything on your plates. You want to stay well and strong."

---

2. "Don't put anything into your ear, Bob," said Mother. "I know a boy who did that. Do you know what happened to him? He could never hear again. You don't want that to happen to you."

---

3. "No," said Mrs. Green. "This isn't Mrs. Pike. No, it is not. This is Mrs. Green talking. You do not have the right telephone number. This is 555-2222. What number do you want?"

---

4. "Let's run," said Dot. "Let's run home. The first one who gets there will win. Tom, you can count. Count to three. When you say three, we will both start running."

1. From the story you can tell that—

    (A) Mother is pleased with the children

    (B) Mother is angry at the children

    (C) the farmer put the food in a basket

2. From the story you can tell that—

    (A) Bob went for a ride in the boat

    (B) Mother went to see Bob and Father

    (C) Bob wasn't thinking

3. From the story you can tell that—

    (A) no one saw Mrs. Green at the store

    (B) someone wanted to talk with Mrs. Pike

    (C) Jan went to see the new store

4. From the story you can tell that—

    (A) Ron did not want to run

    (B) the winner will get a prize

    (C) Dot will not count

1. Ed and Sue said, "Let's put candles on the cake. We can put all the gifts on the table. Everyone is going to play games and have lots of fun."

---

2. "Hold on to your hats," said Aunt May. "The wind is very strong. Hold on tightly, children. The wind will blow your hats away. It will blow them into the water. You won't get them back."

---

3. "My horse can jump over that," said Peg. "It can jump over that two-foot wall. Come on, Star!" she said. "You can do it. You can jump over it. You can jump twice that high."

---

4. "Don't eat so fast," said Mother. "Take your time, Pat. You don't need to eat so fast. It's not good for you. You will get sick if you don't eat more slowly. You'll have time to play."

1. From the story you can tell that—

   (A) two friends are planning a trip

   (B) there will be a birthday party

   (C) a family is at the circus

---

2. From the story you can tell that—

   (A) Aunt May is wearing a hat

   (B) Aunt May likes the wind

   (C) Aunt May knows what the wind can do

---

3. From the story you can tell that—

   (A) Star doesn't know how to jump

   (B) Star can jump four feet high

   (C) Mother gave her coat to a friend

---

4. From the story you can tell that—

   (A) Pat wants to get sick

   (B) Jan saw Pat looking out the door

   (C) Pat wants to play

1. The Bell family wanted a summer house in the mountains. "Let's build a log house," they said. Trucks brought the logs. Everyone in the family worked hard. They worked until they had finished the house.

2. "Come out," said Les. "Come out here. Come out, everyone. Look! Look at this. My hen has a surprise. She has four eggs for us. We can each have an egg to eat."

3. Something jumped. It jumped out of the water. Then it fell back. It made a great big splash. "Did you see that big fish?" asked Father. "Let's go fishing here."

4. After dinner the family went outside. "Look up at the sky," said Pat. "It is filled with tiny lights. I can see the moon."

1. From the story you can tell that—

    (A) the Bells did not want to leave the city

    (B) everyone began to cut down trees

    (C) the family worked well together

2. From the story you can tell that—

    (A) Les is willing to share things

    (B) Mother got a letter from Grandmother

    (C) Les doesn't like the hen

3. From the story you can tell that—

    (A) Father did not want to fish

    (B) a fish made the splash

    (C) Father was alone

4. From the story you can tell that—

    (A) Pat was watching TV

    (B) it was night

    (C) Pat couldn't see in the dark

A. Exercising Your Skill

Read each riddle. Look for clues to help you find the answer. Write your answer on the line.

There are numbers on me.
Sometimes I ring.
You talk into me.
What am I?

_____

I can take you for a ride.
People stop, look, and listen as I go by.
I have many cars.
I go on a track.
What am I?

_____

I help you stay dry.
I come out when it rains.
You hold me over your head.
What am I?

_____

B. Expanding Your Skill

Make up some riddles of your own about the words in the box. Have your class answer the riddles.

fish	sneakers	apple	kite

Make up riddles about other words that you think up yourself.

C. Exploring Language

On your paper, copy each story below. Fill in the blanks with your own words. Pick words that tell about the thing named at the top of each story.

Shark
I live in the _____ .
My teeth are _____ .
I can _____ .

Airplane
I fly high in the _____ .
I have two _____ .
Inside me are _____ .

Tree
I have many _____ .
My branches are _____ .
I grow in the _____ .

Bear
My paws are _____ .
My fur is _____ .
I live in the _____ .

D. Expressing Yourself

Do one of these things.

1. Pretend to be something else. You might be a tree, a horse, or anything you like. Act like this thing. Let the class guess what you are.

2. Make a class riddle book. Get one riddle from each person in the class. Write them in a book. Share your riddles with children in other classes.

3. Get something small. Don't let anyone see what you have. Hide it in a paper bag. Let others ask questions to guess what it is. Answer each question **Yes** or **No**.

1. "Come in here," said Grandmother. "It is raining. You are not wearing your raincoats. You will all get wet. Come in and get dry. You must hurry. You might catch a cold."

---

2. "Look!" cried the children. "A house is on fire down the street. Let's call the firefighters," they said. The children ran into their house. "We must call the firehouse right away," they said.

---

3. "Some children are after me," said Lee. "They want to hit me. They are looking for me. They are trying to find me. Where can I go? Where can I go so they won't find me?"

---

4. "Wait until after dinner, Juan," said Mother. "Don't eat your cake now. You won't want dinner. Eat all your dinner. Eat every bite. Then I will give you cake."

1. From the story you can tell that—

    (A) Grandmother is speaking to one person
    (B) Grandmother is speaking to more than one person
    (C) Grandmother does not care

2. From the story you can tell that—

    (A) the children didn't know what to do
    (B) the children did the right thing
    (C) they got a book about dolls

3. From the story you can tell that—

    (A) Lee is afraid of the children
    (B) the children helped Lee find the dog
    (C) Lee thinks the children are good friends

4. From the story you can tell that—

    (A) dinner was not over
    (B) Juan did not like cake
    (C) Juan was playing ball

1.   "Father and Tom have already left for the game," said Mother. "They did not think you were coming. Dot, I am going shopping. I will be going near the game. I will take you there."

_____

2.   "Do you know what I need?" asked Les. "I need some shoes. Just look at my shoes! I think that my shoes are too small. I need new red shoes. Will you get them for me?"

_____

3.   "I can't find my hat," said Grandfather. "Where did I put it? I had my hat when I came in. Where could it be? I don't want to go out without it. It must be here."

_____

4.   "Pat," said Mother, "your mouth is full. Do not speak. It is not polite. It isn't polite to speak with your mouth full. Wait until you swallow your food. Then you may speak."

1. From the story you can tell that—

   (A) Tom was left behind
   (B) Mother wanted to see the game
   (C) Dot wanted to see the game

2. From the story you can tell that—

   (A) Les likes the color red
   (B) Les has a new friend
   (C) Jan gave Les a red hat

3. From the story you can tell that—

   (A) Grandfather is looking for a coat
   (B) Grandfather is inside
   (C) Jan saw her mother in school

4. From the story you can tell that—

   (A) Pat was doing something wrong
   (B) Mother did not speak to Pat
   (C) it was time to go to sleep

1.   The class visited a bug zoo. "You may hold some of the animals," said the teacher, picking up a caterpillar. Some of the children only wanted to watch. Other children liked to hold and play with the bugs.

---

2.   "You must learn to count," said Mother. "Then you can count money. You can go to the store. You can buy things. You will know if you have the right change."

---

3.   "Where is the picture?" asked Father. "I can't find the picture of the children. Where is it? Mother had it not long ago. Then she let Ms. Hall see it. Where is it now?"

---

4.   "Here is a birthday card from Grandfather. It was sent by airmail," said Mother. "He also sent you some money. Why don't you write him a letter? Write and thank him. Thank him for the card. Thank him for the money."

1. From the story you can tell that—

   (A) the bug zoo was closed

   (B) the teacher did not like to hold the bugs

   (C) some children didn't want to hold the bugs

2. From the story you can tell that—

   (A) Peg asked Mother for money

   (B) Mother knows arithmetic is important

   (C) Peg rode her bicycle

3. From the story you can tell that—

   (A) Father didn't want the picture

   (B) Mother had the picture before Ms. Hall

   (C) no one may play after school

4. From the story you can tell that—

   (A) Grandfather did not send a card

   (B) Grandfather does not live nearby

   (C) Mother had a party for Bob

1. "Children, you can water the grass," said Mother. "Just be careful. Watch what you are doing. Make sure you do not get water on anyone. Do a good job. Then I will have a surprise for you."

2. "My horse can run a long way," said Ron. "I think it can run farther than your horse, Pat. Let's find out. Let's see which horse can run all the way back to the barn."

3. "Look," said Father. "Look at the boat, Jan. Look at the water coming in. See the big hole. We must get back to land. We must get back fast. We may have to swim back to land."

4. "I hope I can start the car," said Mother. "It is very cold this morning." At last Mother got it started. "That's good," said Mother. "I never thought it would start on such a cold morning."

1. From the story you can tell that—

   (A) there may be people near the grass

   (B) Mother made a cake

   (C) Mother did not warn the children

---

2. From the story you can tell that—

   (A) Pat saw Ann at the store

   (B) the children were in the house

   (C) the children were far from the barn

---

3. From the story you can tell that—

   (A) the boat was about to sink

   (B) Jan gave Pat a toy boat

   (C) the boat was red and green

---

4. From the story you can tell that—

   (A) Mother didn't get the car started

   (B) cars don't always start when it's cold

   (C) Mother helped Les catch the puppy

1. "Pat, you were talking last night," said Mother. "You were talking in your sleep. I could make out some of the words. You said something about going to a party."

_____

2. "I don't know how to swim," said Jan. "Will you show me how to swim, Les? I want to learn to swim. Then I could teach Ron and Lee."

_____

3. Sam's hands were cold. They began to hurt. He ran home. "Your hands will be all right," said Mother. "Soon they will stop hurting. Next time remember to wear your gloves."

_____

4. "Where is the telephone book?" asked Lee. "I can't find it. How can I find the number? How can I know what number to call? I wish that someone would help me look for the telephone book."

1. From the story you can tell that—

   (A) Lee liked the elephants best

   (B) Pat never talks while sleeping

   (C) Pat went to sleep before Mother

---

2. From the story you can tell that—

   (A) Jan can swim very well

   (B) Les knows how to swim

   (C) Pat went to see Jan and Lee

---

3. From the story you can tell that—

   (A) Sam forgot something

   (B) Sam's feet hurt

   (C) Father came home

---

4. From the story you can tell that—

   (A) Ron and Jan were in town all day

   (B) Lee knows the telephone number

   (C) Lee didn't know the telephone number

1. "The water is clear today," said the diver. "You can see all the way to the bottom. You can see plants and fish. I will go down there to look at them. Watch me."

---

2. "I'll be right there," said Mother. Mother went to the door. She opened the door. She saw someone running. She didn't see who it was. "Who would ring the bell and run away?" asked Mother.

---

3. "I don't like the picture," said Father. "I don't think it looks like you, Bob. I don't like it. No one thinks that it looks like you. We will just have to try again."

---

4. Ann batted the ball hard. "Run, run," the players yelled at her. "You can make it." Ann ran as fast as she could. "Hooray!" the team shouted.

UNIT 18

1. From the story you can tell that—

   (A) you cannot always see the bottom
   (B) the diver is in a boat
   (C) the diver is on a bridge

---

2. From the story you can tell that—

   (A) someone played a trick on Mother
   (B) Father gave Mother a new dress
   (C) Mother didn't answer the door

---

3. From the story you can tell that—

   (A) Father thinks it's a good picture
   (B) Dot went for a ride with Mother
   (C) Bob will have another picture taken

---

4. From the story you can tell that—

   (A) Ann's team lost the game
   (B) Ann was playing baseball
   (C) Ann was playing tag

1. "How do you know what the sign says?" asked Grandmother. "It's so far away. I can't read it. How can you read it, Les? It's so small. I can't read it from this far away."

---

2. "Where is my shoe?" asked Father. "Who has taken my shoe?" Then he looked at Nip. Now he knew. He knew what had happened. Nip had taken it. The dog had the shoe in its mouth.

---

3. "Let's play hide-and-seek," said Tom. "We can get Peg to play," he said. "We can get Ron. They can ask some of their friends to play. I'll ask Sam if he wants to play."

---

4. "Why are you up so early?" asked Mother. "Why are you up at five o'clock in the morning, Rosa? This isn't any time to be up. You should be in bed. You should be sleeping."

1. From the story you can tell that—

    (A) the sign is very big

    (B) Les can see better than Grandmother

    (C) Grandmother gave the boat to Les

2. From the story you can tell that—

    (A) Father was pleased with Nip

    (B) Father drove Nip to school

    (C) Nip liked to pick things up

3. From the story you can tell that—

    (A) Tom wants many people to play

    (B) the girls can't find the wagon

    (C) Tom doesn't want to play

4. From the story you can tell that—

    (A) Rosa got up very late

    (B) Mother must have been up early

    (C) Rosa went to the store

A. Exercising Your Skill

Look at the map below. It shows what is at a birthday party.

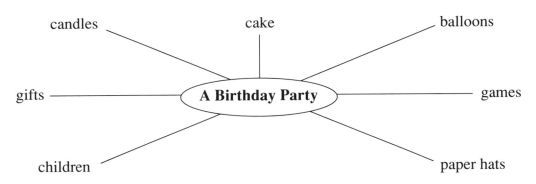

On your paper, draw the map below. Decide what the map is about. Then fill in the circle.

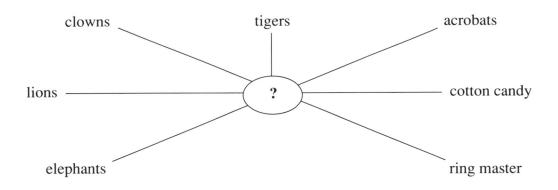

B. Expanding Your Skill

Make your own map. You can make a map of one of the things in the box. Or you can make a map of something else that you think of yourself.

puppet show	parade	swimming pool
music lesson	bus ride	Thanksgiving dinner

C. Exploring Language

Think about the stories below. On your paper, finish each story. Write the last sentence. Tell what the people are going to do.

1.   Mona and Joel got out the tent. They put their sleeping bags in the car. Mom and Dad packed boxes of food for the trip. When everything was ready, the family drove off.

    _____

2.   Paco sat at a table near the window. He could hear his stomach growl. "I can't wait to place my order," he thought. Soon a woman asked, "May I help you, sir?"

    _____

3.   Maria tied her sneakers well. Then she stepped up to the white line to join the other young people. A large crowd looked on. Someone shouted, "On your mark. Get set. Go!" _____

D. Expressing Yourself

Do one of these things.

1. Plan a breakfast, lunch, or dinner. Draw each food you will serve. Can others who look at your picture tell what meal you planned?

2. With others from your class, take turns telling stories. Tell about what you like to do at certain times of the year. Do not tell what time of year you are thinking of. See if others can tell from the clues you give.

1. "I never saw so many cars," said Father. "There are just too many. We seem to stop, stop, stop. That's all we seem to do. It's going to take us a long time to get home."

---

2. It was a picture of a little girl. It was very old. Nan found it under a rug. Nan asked who it was. "Look closely," said Father. "That is your mother. It is a picture of her when she was your age."

---

3. "Hello," said Dale. "Yes, this is the Adams' house. Who is calling? Oh! Mother told me you called before. Will you be able to go with us on Saturday?"

---

4. "I'll find the others," said Jan. "They think they can hide from me. I can find them. I know where they always go. Come out everyone. Come out of the car. I see all of you in there."

1. From the story you can tell that—

   (A) Father was happy to see so many cars

   (B) someone was with Father in the car

   (C) Jean asked Father to buy a pony

---

2. From the story you can tell that—

   (A) the picture had been lost

   (B) Nan looked like her mother

   (C) Nan was late for school

---

3. From the story you can tell that—

   (A) the caller will leave a message

   (B) Dale doesn't know what to say

   (C) no one is at home

---

4. From the story you can tell that—

   (A) Jan doesn't try to find anyone

   (B) the children use an old hiding place

   (C) the family will go out to eat

1. Ed carefully took something green out of his pocket. "Watch it hop," he said. "I found it down by the pond after school. Look at its long legs. I hope Dad will let me keep it."

---

2. "Nancy," said Father, "the telephone is ringing. Will you please answer it? I'm in the shower. I can't come out. Answer the phone, Nan. Answer it before it stops ringing."

---

3. "Help!" cried the children. "Someone help us. A big dog is after us. It wants to bite us. It saw us running and it ran after us. We can see it coming down the street. Help!"

---

4. "I can't wait to see the pictures," said Father. "They will be back soon. I took them more than a week ago. We will see them soon. I'm sure the children will like to see their pictures."

1. From the story you can tell that—

   (A) Ed found a rabbit

   (B) Ed will show the thing to Dad

   (C) snakes live near ponds

2. From the story you can tell that—

   (A) Nan does not like books

   (B) Nan is using the telephone

   (C) Father wants Nan to use the telephone

3. From the story you can tell that—

   (A) the children like the big dog

   (B) the children ran after the cat

   (C) the big dog isn't far away

4. From the story you can tell that—

   (A) Sue went to the store with Tim

   (B) the children are in the picture

   (C) the picture was taken two days ago

1.   "Jo is looking for the ball," said Todd. "I'll hide it. I'll hide it in the backyard. I'll put it in back of the tree. I don't think Jo will look there."

---

2.   "The house is on fire!" shouted Maria. "The fire is too big to put out. I will call the firehouse to get help. Trucks with ladders and hoses will come. People with fire hats and suits will put out the fire."

---

3.   "Why is it so cold in here?" asked the teacher. "This room is very cold. I never knew it to be so cold. I just don't know why. Is that window open? It must have been left open last night."

---

4.   "Look at your hands, Sam," said Mother. "I have never seen your hands look like that. Get them clean right now. How could you sit down to eat with hands as dirty as yours?"

1. From the story you can tell that—

    (A) Todd and Jo run to meet Dad

    (B) Todd wants Jo to find the ball

    (C) Todd doesn't think Jo will find the ball

2. From the story you can tell that—

    (A) Maria will call the firefighters

    (B) Maria put out the fire

    (C) Maria drives a truck

3. From the story you can tell that—

    (A) everyone put the food into the car

    (B) the teacher thinks they forgot to close the window

    (C) the teacher opened the doors and windows

4. From the story you can tell that—

    (A) Sam's hands are clean most of the time

    (B) Mother likes to see dirty hands

    (C) Sam got a chair for Mother

1. "Oh, what a funny picture!" said Tim. "I never saw such a funny picture. What did you draw, Pat? Is it a picture of a house? Is it a dog? What a funny-looking picture!"

---

2. Lee said, "Look, everyone, I have a big fish. See how my pole bends." Lee pulled and pulled. Then the "fish" came out of the water. It was not a fish. It was only an old tire. Everyone laughed.

---

3. "Don't run," said Father. "How many times have I said not to run in the house? Mother has told you. I have told you. I don't want to see you run again, Bob."

---

4. "There's the store," said Jo. "It's down the street. It will open this week. On the day it opens everyone will get a surprise. What do you think I'll get, Sam?"

UNIT 23

1. From the story you can tell that—

   (A) Tim thinks the picture is very good

   (B) Pat can't draw very well

   (C) Jan asked Pat to come out and play

2. From the story you can tell that—

   (A) Lee was fooled

   (B) Lee walked home

   (C) people felt sorry for Lee

3. From the story you can tell that—

   (A) Bob had run in the house before

   (B) Father was happy to see Bob run

   (C) Jan couldn't find the right house

4. From the story you can tell that—

   (A) Sam had no time to paint the toys

   (B) Jo will be at the new store when it opens

   (C) Jo won't go to the new store at all

1. Father and James planned to go to the zoo last weekend. They didn't go on Saturday because it was cold and rainy. It rained all day on Sunday, too. James felt sad.

_____

2. "Where did my ball go?" Kim asked. She looked and looked. She could not find it. Then she looked up at a tree. A squirrel had the ball. The squirrel thought it was something to eat.

_____

3. "My eyes are blue," said Al. "So are Bud's eyes. Let me look at your eyes, Mother. Yours are blue, too. Let's see Father's eyes. His eyes are green. I wish my eyes were green."

_____

4. "When I grow up," said Sarah, "I want to fly an airplane. It must be fun to fly over the towns. It must be fun to look down and see all the people down there."

1. From the story you can tell that—

   (A) they stayed at home on Sunday

   (B) a zoo is fun in the rain

   (C) they did not go to the zoo

2. From the story you can tell that—

   (A) Kim had lost her ball

   (B) squirrels eat balls

   (C) the train brought Grandmother

3. From the story you can tell that—

   (A) Bud didn't take the books with him

   (B) Al liked blue eyes the best

   (C) Al liked green eyes the best

4. From the story you can tell that—

   (A) Jack went to see Grandmother

   (B) Sarah doesn't mind high places

   (C) Sarah wants to be a doctor

1.   "Look in the paper," said Dad. "Look in the newspaper. Can you guess who there is a picture of? Look here. Fran's picture is in the newspaper. Isn't this a nice surprise!"

_____

2.   "Be quiet," said Mother. "If you want to make noise, go outside. The baby is sleeping. Go outside. In a little while the baby will wake up. Then you can come inside to play."

_____

3.   Pat said, "Nell is a family friend who lives next door. Nell drives me to school every day. She helps me do my homework. Last week she showed me how to fix my bike."

_____

4.   "I need a place to put my books," said Les. "These empty boxes will hold them. I can put one on top of the other. My books will be together and easy to reach."

1. From the story you can tell that—

    (A) Dad gave Fran a ride in the car

    (B) Dad did not know about Fran's picture ahead of
        time

    (C) Dad didn't like the picture

2. From the story you can tell that—

    (A) Mother never likes noise

    (B) Mother likes noise

    (C) Mother wants the baby to rest

3. From the story you can tell that—

    (A) Nell is in Pat's class at school

    (B) Pat likes to do homework

    (C) Nell is very helpful to Pat

4. From the story you can tell that—

    (A) boxes can be used to make a bookcase

    (B) books belong in a library

    (C) the boxes were full of food

A. Exercising Your Skill

Read each poem. Tell what word is missing. Each missing word names a job.

> If you want to be a _____
> You must like the air up high.
> For if you have this job
> You'll be flying in the sky.
>
> Would you rather be a _____ ?
> We would get our food from you.
> You would plant the seeds and milk the cows.
> And raise some chickens, too.
>
> How about being a _____ ?
> They are found in all the schools.
> Not only do they teach you,
> They help make all the rules.

B. Expanding Your Skill

Think about each place below. Who works there? What else would you find there? Write the name of each place. Under each place list people and things you would find there. Use words from the box. Add other words you think of.

School	Hospital	Ranch
_____	_____	_____
_____	_____	_____

horses	books	cowboys
doctors	teachers	beds

C. Exploring Language

Some people are knocking on your door. Find out what the people want. On your paper, finish the last sentence of each story.

1.   The first person holds a long rubber hose in one hand. In the other hand, he carries a hatchet. He wears a long rubber raincoat and hat. He is a _____ .

2.   The second person carries a large bag filled with letters. She has parked her red, white, and blue truck on your street. She is holding a package with your name on it. She is a _____ .

3.   The third person pulls up in a long truck. Someone helps him carry out a new kitchen table and four chairs. He is knocking on your door because he wants _____ .

4.   The fourth person drives up in a large white van that makes a loud noise. With another person, she rushes to your door. She is helping to carry a stretcher. She will help take someone to the _____ .

D. Expressing Yourself

Do one of these activities.

1. With a partner, act out the stories in Part C. What does the person who comes to the door say? What do you say? What happens next?

2. Choose a job to act out for your class. You might be a teacher, a doctor, a dishwasher, or a bus driver. Think of other jobs you could act out. Act out the job you choose, alone or with a helper. See if the rest of the class can tell what job you are doing.